I0423494

Relaxation And Stress Reduction Through Home Maintenance

How To Maintain A Clean And Tidy House To Eliminate Unnecessary Stress From Your Life

Table of Contents

Introduction

I want to thank you and congratulate you for purchasing the book *Relaxation And Stress Reduction Through Home Maintenance*.

This book contains proven steps and strategies on how to organize your home and reduce stress brought on by a disorderly room.

How often have you felt all muddled up inside because the house is in complete disarray? No matter what you do, nothing seems to be working to keep your house clean and orderly. Chances are, you are simply picking up after all the chaos and arranging your items in exactly the same way as before. In this book, you'll learn a completely new organization technique that can permanently keep your house orderly.

With the information provided here, you'll only need a few minutes each day to tackle all the home organizing chores, giving you more time to focus on the important aspects of daily living. From bedroom to kitchen, find out how to completely change the way you view your home!

Chapter 1: De-stress and De-clutter

A lot of people notice that coming home to a cluttered, messy house prevents them from experiencing full-on relaxation. This isn't really surprising considering how the cluttered surroundings tend to affect the brain, making it lose concentration and prompting it to constantly worry about the state of its environment.

This phenomenon isn't even specific from one person to another. Studies reveal that the brain itself relies on proper organization to enhance mental acuity and memory. It's called "clustering," and whenever the brain wants to remember a set of information, it usually "clusters" it into groups to make the memory more distinct. That's why we often separate long sequences of numbers with a hyphen (-) in an effort to group them together.

Hence, disorganized surroundings with no definite "cluster" actually mess with the brain. This is why you shouldn't be surprised at how frustrated you get when the house is in disarray, and you're having problems remembering small things or focusing on specific tasks. It's not you – it's probably your surroundings.

That being said, here's how you can start rearranging your life by de-cluttering and reorganizing your possessions. In this first chapter, we'll talk about the different ways you can go about throwing some stuff away without regretting it later on.

Have you used it in the past year?

This is the biggest and most solid test for deciding whether you should keep or throw away some of your stuff. Think back to the last 365 days and start separating your stuff into two boxes: discard and undecided. The undecided pile is for the stuff you can't bear losing and may need a little more decision time on your part. Within the next 1 to 3 months, the Undecided box should be whittled down to nothing. For now though, you should be happy with the current state of things.

The great thing about the 365-day test is that it doesn't exclude the items you use once a year – like the Christmas tree or the special Thanksgiving China. A minimalist would tell you to discard all this stuff because you don't *need* it, but if you're just trying to de-clutter your life, then it's perfectly acceptable to keep that turkey baster. Go through different rooms in the house, filling up your boxes along the way. Don't worry about leaving the room in a mess after you're done deciding which items to throw out. The materials left behind will be the ones you get to organize later on.

Sell It Off!

The biggest problem for most people after completing their Discard box is what to do about the stuff once you've chosen to get rid of it. You should not just throw it in the trash – especially if a lot of those items are still useful. The best answer to this problem is to sell off whatever you have left behind by picking the items that you feel will fetch a good price in the market.

Yard sales are old school, but they can still be useful if you're partial to them. The internet, however, is your best friend. Try to sell your stuff locally to avoid all the hassle of shipping to who-knows-where. Don't forget to be careful when selling locally, though – make sure you exchange items in a public place and not in your home. Some of the websites where you can pull off a sale include eBay and Craigslist. You can also utilize Facebook, Twitter and other social media websites, depending on where you believe you'll find a buyer.

If you're not sure of the value of the product, check online for comparison. The beauty here is that since you're not trying to make a profit, you can sell those items off at a lower cost than the competition, ensuring that people are willing to buy them immediately.

Belongs in the Trash

Some items you have no other choice but to trash. These are basically non-salvageable materials or those that are way past their sell-by date. You might be surprised at just how many of these items you have in the house. Aside from food, beauty products and medications are other items you need to get rid of if they're past their expiration date. Note though, that most medications require a specific method of disposal, so make sure to check before throwing them in the bin.

Donate and Give Away

If you're feeling more generous, try giving away your stuff to friends, family, neighbors, and people who you know could use the items. There's really no shortage of possible recipients for this!

Recycle

Recycling some of your junk is also an option, but unless you're a pro at this or the instructions are incredibly easy, it's best not to try out this method. Sure, you could help with the environment by recycling old stuff (like turning old CD's into an aesthetic box), but if you're not used to the process then you just might botch up the procedure. If you're dealing with olds newspapers, bottles and the like, however, just drive to your nearest recycling plant and give them away for further processing.

Storage

You can also try storing some items, either in the attic or by hiring a small storage facility for all your surplus items. This idea is not recommended though, since at some point, you'd find yourself opening the box and possibly taking out all the "junk" that clutters your home, putting you back right at square one. A storage facility can also be costly and unnecessary if you're not really keeping anything expensive. With that being said, try to avoid storing anything from your cluttered home, and instead, decide to discard them for good or keep them for good.

Those are your options! The question is what do you do with everything that's been left behind? Let's take this one room at a time. Here are some tricks and organizational ideas you can try out. Remember, you're allowed to experiment as much as you want so feel free to make some changes to the suggestions here!

Chapter 2: Bed and Bathroom

Your bedroom is your most private sanctuary, so it's important to have it properly organized with everything you need within reach. With the place free and clear of chaos, you will find yourself achieving a greater sense of relaxation when lounging in your inner sanctuary.

Closet

The closet is probably the most disorganized part of every bedroom. You try to stack your clothes properly every Sunday only to find it in complete disarray by Friday. This happens because by folding the clothes in the usual way, you're basically creating a "stack" that easily falls down when you grab one of the clothes from the bottom. To prevent this from happening, imagine your closet as a suitcase. When packing clothes in a suitcase, you are advised to roll them up and arrange them horizontally so that you'd be able to see all the clothes from the top. This way, you also won't disturb everything when you pull one of them out, ensuring you retain an organized-looking closet for good! Remember, at this point your closet should already be whittled down to the stuff you actually wear. Apply the 365-day rule when reducing your clothes to the barest essentials.

Television

If at all possible, do not put the television in the bedroom. Although you may love watching TV, studies show this can contribute to insomnia for most people. Confine the TV to the living room and find yourself getting better sleep every night.

Arrange Clothes by Occasion

People typically have a unique way of arranging their clothes, but if your current method doesn't seem to be working, perhaps it's time to take a new approach. A good technique is to keep the "home," "party," and "work" clothes separate. You can try folding the home clothes and then hanging the work and party clothes. To separate the two, try putting a marker in between the clothesline, telling you exactly where the clothes are supposed to go. Some people go so far as to arrange the clothes depending on color, length, and style. Either way, a basic arrangement should be an excellent way to start your more orderly life.

Accessories

Women especially have a box full of accessories from bracelets, rings, earrings, necklaces, and even all kinds of ties and ribbons. Try to sort through all of these, discarding the ones that don't match anything, especially the multi-colored ones that are tough to coordinate with a lot of outfits. Your case of accessories should contain items you can use for multiple occasions and that only need to be mixed and matched depending on the situation. Keep in mind that bracelets and necklaces tend to tangle together, so it's best to hang them for storage.

Organize Based on Frequency of Use

Arrange your bedroom items based on how often you need them. For example, your favorite tube of lipstick can be kept on top of the vanity where you can just grab it, apply and go. The same rule applies for anything you use on a daily basis such as eyeliner, mascara, powder and various other items you might need. For items that you use regularly but not on a daily basis (like tampons), you can keep them in a lower compartment of your cabinet. This way, it does not block access to all the daily items.

Assess Possible Storage Space

Take a good look at your bedroom, and consider possible storage spaces you don't really use. A lot of people seem to discount areas like beneath the bed, above the headboard, the inside of closet doors, and more. Try to check out these places and consider what can be placed there that offers easy access. For example, beneath the bed you can place a roller to keep all your reading materials in. This way, you can simply roll in and roll out the book when you're done with it at night. You can also utilize hanging organizers inside the closet doors, putting in pairs of socks, panties, and handkerchiefs to allow for easy access. Plus, this minimizes the chances of losing socks amid the mountain of clothes.

Buy Storage as Needed

It's really not advisable to buy more stuff if you're trying to de-clutter your bedroom. However, if you've carefully assessed your bedroom and noted that some items will work better in specific personal storage units, then don't hesitate to make that purchase. Keep in mind though that (1) the storage unit should fit nicely in the room and (2) it should be able to store all the extra items you have lying around.

Medicine Cabinet

Bathrooms are a bit trickier to handle because they're usually the smallest room in the house. If you have a small bathroom, you don't want to bring the walls in any closer by installing a medicine cabinet. Instead, you can use your nightstand's drawer for keeping the medications you use on a regular basis. For the bathroom, you can try hanging a thinner mirror that takes up less space.

Back of the Door

Another wonderful place you can take advantage of in the bathroom (or any other room, for that matter) is the back of the door. Use it to hang clear shoe compartments where you can place your bathroom paraphernalia like shaving cream, cleanser, toner, exfoliants, toothbrush, and various other items that you might need. If the door is big enough, you can also use the top space to hang your towels. The possibilities are endless once you've figured out exactly what needs to be done!

Trim the Shower Curtain

If you have a shower curtain that drags all the way down the tub, perhaps it's a good idea to trim the bottom part just enough to ensure privacy when using the shower. A trimmed shower curtain prevents mold buildup, plus it actually makes the floor look cleaner and more organized.

Toilet Paper

A great way to make sure you never run out of toilet paper is to keep a supply of it nearby. Use a clear umbrella stand for this job, preferably something that protects the paper from getting wet. You could probably stock 3 or more within the stand, plus the one that's already in placc on the toilet paper holder. This way, you'll know exactly when the paper is running out, and you can add more supply to the emergency stack.

Overhead Cabinets and Racks

Use some basic IKEA furniture to install overhead cabinets in the bathroom, allowing you more space for supplies without compromising the small floor area. You can store towels, toilet paper, shampoo, and small knick-knacks in this space, ensuring you always have enough every time you walk in the bathroom. Note that although the cabinets must be overhead, they should be low enough that you can reach anything you need. This spot would also be perfect for bathroom cleaning supplies you don't want the kids to reach.

BEDROOMS should have 3 to 5 floor furniture, which includes the bed, nightstand, vanity, closet and cabinets. Storage shelves that hang do not count, so you can put as many as you want if you find yourself lacking in space.

As for the **BATHROOM,** your furniture should be limited to just one or two items occupying the floor area. Keep small items hidden in cabinets and drawers while putting frequently used items within easy reach.

Chapter 3: Avoiding Kitchen Disasters

The kitchen usually contains too many things at once, causing problems for most homeowners. You'll find yourself dealing with half a dozen plates, dozens of spoons and forks, a dozen mugs and so much more. Unfortunately, most of these items are haphazardly placed in cabinets as they are taken out and used. How do you approach this particular problem? The following are some orderly tips when it comes to kitchen disasters:

Clean and Empty

Start opening up your kitchen cabinets and reorganizing the items you find there. If you have enough space, it's usually a good idea to store all your frequently used items in just one cabinet so that you don't have to start opening them one by one when preparing dinner. For example, if there are just three or four of you routinely eating in the kitchen, then arrange four plates, four glasses, and four pairs of spoons and forks in one kitchen cabinet. The overflowing utensils can be kept in other cabinets for storage, just in case you host a party. The great thing about this is that you will not be tempted to stack dishes in the sink or take your plate all over the house. With just a limited number of utensils to work with, you can be sure that after every meal, the dishes are washed and returned to their proper place.

Keep It Transparent

One of the biggest reasons why kitchen containers become disorderly after one week of straightening it out is the "on and off" process of checking the lids. Chances are when looking for something, you tend to open a container to check inside, close it, and then put it back haphazardly. Do this several times a day and it isn't surprising to find your kitchen cabinets suddenly looking like a storm went through them. Prevent this from happening by using transparent containers. This way, you know the contents and do not have to "guess" the items. If you don't have the budget to purchase a whole set of transparent containers, however, then at least invest in a label maker. This way, you can group kitchen items together and simply use the labels as a guiding post when looking for something.

Grouping Items

Group kitchen items that can be spilled or messy when not handled correctly. This may include honey, jam, condiments, and more. Try to keep them in an easy-to-clean container like a Lazy Susan – preferably something you can wipe or wash to clean. By doing so, you can contain kitchen messes to just one area, keeping the rest of the room clean and easy to manage.

Corner Storage

Another good use for the Lazy Susan is corner storage. This way, all you have to do is rotate the tray to reach the farther parts of the cabinet. With this technique, you'll also find it easier to clean the kitchen space and the different items you have.

Keep Items Close

Kitchen items are best placed in locations where you can easily find them. For example, the spice rack can be near the stove, the knives on the counter, the dishwasher near the sink, and more. This is the same principle you use when arranging the bedroom – the only difference are the items you need to arrange.

Check the Food

Check the refrigerator, cleaning out all the food items that might have been stuck in there for a long time. Assess the items inside – are they still good, have they gone bad, or are they nearing spoilage? Throw away the bad ones and use the old, "near-spoiled" items as soon as possible. When buying groceries, it's usually a good idea to purchase items with the farthest expiration dates, especially if you're the kind who tends to forget food in the fridge.

Trash Cans

Having different trashcans for recyclable and biodegradable items is always a good idea, especially if you happen to have a garden where organic fertilizer can be utilized. Ensure there's a trashcan centrally located in the kitchen where you can easily dump items as needed. Most homeowners note that trashcans are a wonderful way to ensure cleanliness in the entire house so try not to confine this to the kitchen alone. Having a trash can near the bedroom door, in the living room and the bathroom works wonders in keeping the house free of messes.

Whiteboard Hack

The refrigerator door is prime real estate you should use to make the kitchen more orderly. Simply place a whiteboard on the upper half of the refrigerator and make a list of the things you do have and the items you need to purchase the next time you visit the grocery store. What's great about this is that you don't have to constantly open the fridge thinking about what to cook with the remaining items inside. Plus, this ensures you will never run out of anything because you know exactly what food items are missing or running low.

Creating Hanging Storage

Choose an area in your kitchen at least 3 feet away from the stove where you can place a peg for hanging items. Use this exclusively for aprons, potholders, and other cloth materials you use often. With the hanging space, you'll find that there's less chance of misplacing the potholders or having them cluttered all over the kitchen.

Use a Hanging Shoe Holder

The plastic shoe holder is an ingenuous way to handle cleaning materials. Try tacking this at the back of your kitchen cabinet for easy access without burning up precious space. By keeping cleaning items out of the way, your kids or pets are less likely to find them.

Sink and Counter Space

In the kitchen, the sink and counter are usually the spaces that see most of the action. That being said, it only makes sense for you to keep these two areas clean and clear at all times. Many homeowners notice that if their sink and counter are free of debris, they make conscious efforts to make sure it stays that way. Even the smallest items shouldn't be left lying around like a spoon or some crumbs. You might tell yourself you'll do it later, but why not now? It usually takes less than 30 seconds to wash a spoon or clear the crumbs off the counter. A good rule of thumb is that if it takes you less than two minutes to accomplish, it's best to just do it *now*.

Magnetic Knife Strip

Ditch the knife slots and opt for a magnetic knife strip, situated high above the sink. What's great about this is you're 100% sure it's out of reach of the kids.

Clean and Prevent Major Problems

The kitchen can be one of the dirtiest parts of the house, and one of the ways to ensure organization is by preventing any major "clean up" problems. Be aware of the different cleaning tricks you can use to quickly fix a dirty kitchen and bring it back into the pristine and organized room you love.

- Clean Your Blender - Having a hard time cleaning your blender? Once you're done using it, fill the compartment with warm water, drop some liquid soap inside, and turn it on. You'll get a wonderfully clean blender without too much effort.

- Clog Prevention - Sink clogging is best prevented rather than fixed when the pipe is already teeming with blockages. To ensure this doesn't happen, just throw in boiling water at least once a week. No need to specially boil water for the job – just use whatever's left when you boil water for tea.

- Coffee Maker – cleaning your coffee maker is pretty much like cleaning a blender. Simply load the water tank with water and add some vinegar into the mix. Plug in the cord and turn on the water, allowing it to do what it does but with the coffee basket empty of any grains. The vinegar in the mix helps dissolve any lingering stains from the coffee and pushes them out into the waiting carafe. When done, just throw the hot water carefully into the sink, so you can de-clog the pipes at the same time.

- Freezer – defrost your freezer at least once every two weeks, depending on how thick the ice happens to be. To create instant space in the freezer, try using magazine racks as shelves.

- Pantyhose Hack – have some old pantyhose lying around? Drape it on a yardstick and run it under the refrigerator and other hard-to-reach places. This instantly cleans tight spaces with zero cost.

- Stainless Steel – try using flour to clean and fix blemishes on your stainless steel materials

- Vanilla – make your kitchen smell great by using vanilla in your oven. Once you've cleaned the oven, use some deodorizer on the rack with just a few drops of vanilla. Wipe them down, turn on the oven and enjoy the wonderful scent!

Note that kitchens are hotspots when it comes to house accidents, so don't forget safety when making the room more organized and functional. Don't try to hang anything near the stove or block the cooling mechanism of any appliance – especially the refrigerator. A fire extinguisher conveniently located nearby is also a must.

Chapter 4: Living Room

As a rule, rooms with televisions in them are heavy-traffic. This is why you'll find that the living room requires a firm hand to organize and maintain. The following are some tips and techniques to get you started:

Pile It Up

Other than the bedroom, the living room is the only place where you can use this technique. Basically, all you have to do is gather all the out-of-place items in the living room and put them into one big pile. Start attacking that pile, categorically replacing the items to their proper spots. If the item doesn't have a "designated" area yet, then make one. For example, remote controls tend to travel from couch to couch in most living rooms. Prevent this from happening by placing a box on the coffee table and designating it as the remote's new home. This comes with the added advantage of never losing the remote again.

Personals and Collections

Collections are best displayed in small quantities, which leaves more room for personal items. To make things more orderly, assign a different spot for personal items (pictures, etc) while putting your collections somewhere else. The beauty of limiting your collection on display is that you have the chance to change it when needed. Shift the items around, remove some favorite pieces, and replace them with new ones until you get a completely different look without too much effort. Keep in mind that you don't want the living room cluttered with too many knick-knacks.

Couch and Pillows

A lot of people don't consider this, but too many pillows can actually be harmful rather than helpful to a space. You'll find that with numerous pillows on the couch, you're creating possible hiding spaces for remotes, keys, toys, and other small items. Instead, limit the number of your pillows to the barest essentials, opting for three or four depending on how many people can fit in your couch. Opting for complementary colors will also go a long way in creating a harmonious and seemingly large space for the living room.

Divided by Function

Divided by function is a technique that works best for the living room, although you can also try using it in the kitchen. Basically, you have to figure out exactly what activities are done in your living room. Is it a playroom, a place where the kids watch TV, where you read, where you receive guests, etc? List what happens in the living room, limiting the room to only five activities. Now, start dividing the living room according to these activities. For example, try to position the sofa for watching TV and then add a magazine rack where people can conveniently reach for some reading material. Some of these functions may overlap but that's okay, as long as each function is conveniently covered by the facilities you have in the room. Remove everything else that does not add value to the space.

Spacing Furniture

Get rid of some furniture, if necessary, while acquiring multipurpose furniture. There are currently furniture items that also function as storage compartments. Ottomans that can be opened, coffee tables with a compartment for magazines and side tables with a cabinet are currently available in many stores. As much as possible, don't try to arrange your furniture close together. Put a few inches of space in between to create the illusion of size. This way, the room looks bigger than it actually is.

Bowls and Boxes

If you're going to display anything in your living room, make sure it's a decorative bowl or a box. It should be large enough to contain keys, mobile phones, and various odds & ends that you tend to leave lying around and promptly forget. You can put it on top of the coffee table and notice how your small items tend to gravitate toward the bowl. You don't even need to put conscious effort into the task – when something small is missing, there's a good chance it's in the bowl.

Flat and Focal

Choose a large flat space in your living room like the coffee table or a piano and utilize it to create a focal point. You can do this by putting something large and eye-catching in the center, making the object seem like it's the "center" of the room. You could try putting a vase with flowers on it, an outstanding figurine, or anything you find aesthetically pleasing. Keep in mind that your focal point is supposed to stand-alone – anything else you put beside it on the flat surface will ruin the balance of the room. With this concept in mind, you should make sure that all small knick-knacks are removed from the flat surface.

Landing Strips

Landing strips are more sophisticated forms of bowls and boxes. This is usually an elongated table placed a few steps away from the door. This is basically where all the things you're carrying around will land once you get inside the house. Most people like to include a bowl in the landing strip to fine tune where your small things will land. For example, you walk into the house carrying groceries and a set of car keys. The landing strip is where you are most likely to put all of this until you're ready to take care of it. For most homeowners, the strip is also a good way to ensure you have everything you need before leaving the house. Just put all the bags and outdoor items on the table and stop by it when you're ready to leave. This way, you will not feel flustered about leaving anything locked inside.

Calendar Display

There's something about a big calendar that puts everything into perspective at home. Try hanging one in a high-traffic area where everyone in your family can see it. The living room is just one example but prime places also include the bedroom (if you live alone) and the kitchen, right beside the refrigerator where you can be sure others will see it. Make sure the calendar is big enough for you to write reminders on specific dates like appointments with the doctors, payment of bills, etc. This will ensure you don't forget about important dates and find yourself scrambling to make the cut.

Invest in a Shoe Rack

A shoe rack is both cheap and useful, providing you with sufficient storage space for outdoor shoes. They are best placed near the door so visitors have somewhere to place them when entering your home. With these racks, not only can you prevent mud tracks but the elevation also helps dry out boots and shoes both inside and outside. When cleaning the floor area, all you have to do is lift the rack a few inches off the ground for a thorough sweep.

Computers and More

Computer can be kept anywhere, but the television, CD player, game console, and other electronics are typically kept in the living room. It doesn't matter what electronics you have; a common problem with this in most homes is the cords. You may always find yourself having to follow each cord to find out which appliance it connects to. Prevent this small but chaotic problem by putting labels at the end of each cord. You can also try buying a cord organizer but why spend money on something you can fix easily with some paper and scotch tape? Be careful though – you don't want the labels to be so long that they tangle in the cords themselves.

Chapter 5: Kids, Pets, and More

Maintaining a clean and orderly house is easy if you live alone. Unfortunately, having kids, pets, and a significant other can put a damper on your home organizational approach. With kids and pets, you might need to tweak your techniques a little so everyone can follow house rules. That being said, the following are some techniques that should help:

Pet Area

Assigning a specific space where your pet eats and sleeps is the first step in ensuring an orderly home even with a cat or dog around. Both animals are capable of understanding the concept of territory and would gladly eat and sleep in the same place every day. Make sure their food bowl is located in the same place all the time. The water bowl should always be filled and placed in the same area of the house. Note that you have to be firm with pets if you don't want them messing up the whole space. Don't let them inside the bedroom or anywhere else they're not supposed to go – not even once. Being lenient once in a while can lead to behavior problems with the pet.

A Box for Doggy Toys

Much like with kids, keeping a box specifically for doggy toys is a must. Offer them to the dog individually on different occasions, so you don't find yourself getting stuck picking up after the pooch. It's also a good idea to make sure everyone in the home understands the limitations you've set when interacting with the family pets.

Establish a Routine

Pets respond best to a routine. Cats are usually simpler because they live indoors, which means all you have to focus on is what time they get to eat. Dogs are a little more complicated. You want to establish the right time for them to eat, go out for a walk, and go to the bathroom. As early as possible, introduce your pup to a routine to limit interruptions during the day. With this approach, you'll find yourself living a more time-efficient existence.

Kids' Toys

When it comes to kids, you really cannot expect yourself to pick up after them after every playtime. Instead, have a big box for their toys, and ask the kids to dump everything inside when they are done. This way, you do not have to worry about putting them all back on their proper shelves. To maintain an organized kid's room, homeowners usually need to strike a deal with the child, assigning them chores or tasks to make sure the room stays as pristine as possible.

Shoes and Clothes for Kids

Kids can grow up so fast! Before you know it, half of their clothes no longer fit and are wasting space in the closet, gathering dust. Most moms have figured out a way to handle this problem. Every time they notice a garment no longer fits the child, they pop it into a box conveniently located near the washroom. When the box is full or contains a number of clothes, they simply take the box to a local charity shop or wherever it might be needed. This way the closet remains updated when it comes to clothes.

Be Involved in the Process

For most kids, their idea of organizing and cleaning their room is to shove things in every possible space until the table, the floor, and the bed are clear of clutter. In many cases, this means just hiding their toys in closets, desk shelves, or under the bed. This is definitely not a good practice, and in time, you might find this bad habit being carried to other parts of the house.

As a parent, one of your goals is to make sure the child understands the concept of organization. To do this, take the time to clean their room with them, showing them where things go and allocating "homes" for their various items. For example, all the toys go in the basket, the books go in the shelf, and the shoes should be kept under the bed or on the shoe rack. Introducing the concept of "homes" will ensure, if things become disarrayed again, your child has a proper idea of what things go where.

Introducing Categories for Children

When teaching your child how to organize, try separating items into categories. This can be something as simple as where the clothes go and where the toys should be placed. You can also try introducing the concept of clean clothes and dirty clothes, specifying where the latter should go and when they should bring them out to be laundered. Some parents like to introduce color sorting into the mix, allowing children to recognize categories based on color. For example, the red basket is where all the toys go, while the blue basket contains all the soiled clothes, etc.

School Items

School bags should be rearranged every night before going to sleep to ensure the child has everything he or she needs before heading to school. This is just a small concern that could ruin a parent's whole day because it delays the rest of the chores that need to be done. Try to establish a specific routine for arranging the child's bag. This way, all he or she has to do is grab the bag before being picked up by the school bus.

Chapter 6: Additional Tips and Maintenance

The following are small things that many homeowners seem to forget when organizing their homes. Check them out one by one, and find out what you might be missing.

Keep Rags On Hand

Always have bits and pieces of cloth ready just in case you need to wipe something. It usually takes less than a minute to sweep the surface of nightstands or coffee table to keep them dust free. The rags should be placed somewhere convenient but not easily seen.

Cleaning Cabinet

We all have a specific cabinet where all the cleaning supplies are kept. What you'll notice however is that the cleaning cabinet itself is disorganized and "unclean." Make sure to fix this problem by using racks, hanging shoe compartments, and boxes to arrange cleaning supplies. Everything must be easily seen once you open the cabinet, so you know when supplies are running low.

Fold Clothes Immediately

Whenever you take clothes out of the dryer, make sure you fold them immediately and put them in the closet. A lot of disorganization problems stem from leaving small chores lying around to be taken care of later. The same rule applies for dishes in the sink.

Papers, Papers, Papers

One of the biggest reasons for clutter in the home is papers in the form of bills, letters, magazines, brochures, and more. It's time to get rid of that stuff. As mentioned in the first chapter, you can try recycling them and contribute to the betterment of the environment. Some papers, however, you just cannot trash or bring to the recycling facility. Deposit slips, payment slips, and various other documents containing sensitive information must be kept in a safe place. Collect these papers and group them by type in a clear envelope. You never really know when you might need them in the future, perhaps when completing your tax returns.

Note that you might still be receiving old school, paper newsletters when emails would do. Cancel subscriptions to these to reduce the amount of junk you receive every day. Most homeowners install a "receiving line" for their mail, usually a small box situated on the landing strip. From here, you can sort out the mail before deciding to go anywhere else.

Using Dividers

Dividers can be something as simple as putting a small box in a cabinet where all your tiny possessions are contained. For example, it could hold your nail cutter, batteries, eyebrow trimmer or whatever material that could easily get lost in your closet. Dividers can be used in practically all containers and can be made out of anything as long as it's flat and durable enough. An excellent example is a shoebox.

Colors

Choosing the correct color for your home goes a long way into making it seem bigger and more organized. A good technique is to paint your walls using the same color, varying only in shades to create distinction between different areas. This works well if you have an open-layout type of house with the colors removing barriers between the spaces. Doing this, you get the feeling of having one big room with multiple functions. Following the color scheme, try to use drapes and furniture that complement or follow the specific pattern. This way, you create a harmonious setting with very little chaotic clashes.

Sheer Drapes

It's almost always better to let natural light inside the house, removing any lingering shadow within the room. With the sun shining so brightly, you will find that even the furthest corner of your home receives adequate lighting. If this isn't possible, try investing in sheer drapes – preferably with the same color as your interior décor. This not only lets the light in but the matching shade of the drapes and home expands the perceived area, making your place seem bigger.

Make Your Living Space Seem Bigger

No matter the size of your living space, there's no question that the way you design it can make it seem bigger or smaller. To achieve a neater and more orderly living space, you want to maximize the area of your room, preventing yourself from putting too many items and making it difficult to do specific tasks indoors. With that said, the following are some techniques you can use to make your space seem as big as possible:

- Mirrors – mirrors are the ultimate tool if you want to make your place look bigger. Prop it somewhere convenient like in your room or the living room to multiply the space. Installing glass or see through dividers can also make the space expand, allowing you to achieve a more open and, therefore, larger look.

- Cantaloupe Rule – the official cantaloupe rule is used by many professionals in the business. Basically, any designs smaller than a cantaloupe do not add to the aesthetic vibe of a home but rather, makes it seem more cluttered. If you want to create a more orderly living space, ditch the small figurines and concentrate on the items bigger than a cantaloupe.

Small Spaces Matter

Take the time to check small spaces as well. The corner table might be small in the grand scheme of things, but it will definitely contribute something to the overall organized appearance of the room. As much as possible, no flat surface should be left cluttered. All small items must be moved out of the way, preferably placed inside cabinets where they are properly arranged. If this is not possible, small containers can help keep the space clean and organized.

Hang Often

Always be on the lookout for spaces where you can hang items. The wall is probably one of the least used parts of the house that is perfect if you want to maximize space. Using this trick, you can hang a lot of things including mugs, pots, pans, knives, cookbooks, spices, and so much more. Use stickers to hang items on the walls as often as possible so that you don't have to damage the walls with holes. This way, if you feel like changing the layout of the room, there's no need to make any major revisions.

Websites for Home Organizing

Every home is different, so your approach should be customized to what you have and what you need. Different websites like Pinterest can provide further home improvement and organization techniques. Get inspiration from these websites and try suggestions in your own home. You can also try checking out IKEA tricks with different furniture and by browsing through different recycled images for inspiration.

Clean as You Go

The ultimate home organization tip: fix things as they happen. Do not let anything stand and wait until you feel like taking care of them. Used a spoon? Wash it. Just finished drying some clothes? Fold and store them immediately. They may seem like simple tasks but choosing not to do them immediately results in a stack of chores that will take hours to complete.

Major Clean Ups

Obviously, you can't clean everything as you move along. The bed sheets have to be changed, the drapes need to be washed and major bouts of cleaning must be done to ensure there's very little buildup of dirt in the home. Most people do this once a week, but if you apply the "clean as you go" rule, you might get away with doing this twice a month or every two weeks. Create a schedule that works for you. Some people like to do all the major jobs in one day while others like to separate them into different days (steam clean on Sunday, wash bed sheets on Monday, etc). Write the schedule down if need be and stick to it as much as possible.

If you have noticed, some of the organizing tips can be contradictory. This is to be expected since people approach organizing in different manners. With this book, however, we hope you have managed to find some organizing techniques that appeal to you. Try using one or more of the strategies presented here, observing yourself for some time and adjusting methods as you see fit.

IMPORTANT!

There's a good chance you won't achieve all your home organizing goals in just one sweep. You might have to do this more than once before you manage to establish a routine that works for you. Don't give up though – an organized home is definitely possible. You just have to find a way that works perfectly with the lifestyle you have.

Conclusion

Thank you again for purchasing this book!

I hope this book was able to help you better assess your home, pinpoint the exact problems, and find the perfect organizational technique needed to keep it in order.

The next step is to try out some of the suggestions mentioned in this book.

Thank you and good luck!